MOY SAND AND GRAVEL

MOY SAND AND GRAVEL

PAUL MULDOON

FARRAR, STRAUS AND GIROUX

NEW YORK

FARRAR, STRAUS AND GIROUX
18 West 18th Street, New York 10011

Distributed in Canada by Douglas & McIntyre Ltd.
Printed in the United States of America
Published in 2002 by Farrar, Straus and Giroux
First paperback edition, 2004

The Library of Congress has cataloged the hardcover edition as follows:
Muldoon, Paul.
    Moy sand and gravel / Paul Muldoon.— 1st ed.
        p.   cm.
    ISBN-13: 978-0-374-21480-7 (hc : alk. paper)
    ISBN-10: 0-374-21480-8 (hc : alk. paper)
    I. Title.

PR6063.U367 M69 2002
821'.914—dc21

                        2002020129

Paperback ISBN-13: 978-0-374-52884-3
Paperback ISBN-10: 0-374-52884-5

Designed by Gretchen Achilles

www.fsgbooks.com

FOR DOROTHY AND ASHER

CONTENTS

MOY SAND AND GRAVEL

HARD DRIVE

With my back to the wall
and a foot in the door
and my shoulder to the wheel
I would drive through Seskinore.

With an ear to the ground
and my neck on the block
I would tend to my wound
in Belleek and Bellanaleck.

With a toe in the water
and a nose for trouble
and an eye to the future
I would drive through Derryfubble

and Dunnamanagh and Ballynascreen,
keeping that wound green.

UNAPPROVED ROAD

I

When we came to the customs post at Aughnacloy, as at Cullaville or
Pettigoe,
I was holding my breath
as if I might yet again be about to go

underwater . . . The fortieth
anniversary of 1916 had somehow fizzled out, the New Year's Eve attack
on Brookeborough ending in the deaths

of O'Hanlon and South, while Dev was likely to bring back
internment without trial . . . As we drew
level with the leveled shack

I was met by another black-coated, long fellow, though he wore a sky-blue
winding-cloth or scarf
wrapped round his mouth and nose, leaving only a slit for him to peer
through.

II

"In the late fifties I was looking for a place," he nestled his coffee cup on its

zarf

and turned to me, thirty years later, in Rotterdam . . .
"An ancestral place . . . A place my ancestors knew as *Scairbh*

na gCaorach." "*Scairbh na gCaorach,*" I chewed on my foul madams,
"is now better known as 'Emyvale'
though the Irish name means 'the sheep-steeps' or 'the rampart of rams.' "

" 'Rampart of rams?' That makes sense. It was the image of an outcrop of

shale

with a particularly sheer

drop that my ancestors, the 'people of the veil,'

held before them as they drove their flocks from tier to tier
through Algeria, Mali, and Libya all the way up to Armagh, Monaghan, and

Louth

with—you'll like this—a total disregard for any frontier."

III

"Patrick Regan?" A black-coated R.U.C. man was unwrapping a scarf from
                                                              his mouth
and flicking back and forth from my uncle's license to his face.
"Have you any news of young Sean South?

The last I heard he was suffering from a bad case
of lead poisoning. Maybe he's changed his name to Gone West?"
I knew rightly he could trace

us by way of that bottle of Redbreast
under my seat, that carton of Players, that bullion chest of butter.
I knew rightly we'd fail each and every test

they might be preparing behind the heavy iron shutters
even now being raised aloft
by men carrying belt saws and blowtorches and bolt cutters.

IV

As he turned to me again, thirty years later in Rotterdam, the Tuareg doffed
his sky-blue scarf. "Back in those days I saw no risk
in sleeping under hedges. As a matter of fact I preferred a thorn hedge to a
                                                                    hayloft

because—you'll like this—it reminded me of the tamarisks
along the salt route into Timbuktu."
He crossed his forearms lightly under his armpits as if he might be about
                                                                    to frisk

himself, then smiled as he handed me the sky-blue
winding-cloth and a clunking water gourd.
"It had been my understanding that *Scairbh na gCaorach* meant 'the
                                                        crossing of ewes'

for *scairbh* means not 'a ledge' but 'a ford' or, more specifically, 'a
                                                        shallow ford.' "
And he immediately set off at a jog trot down an unapproved road
near Aughnacloy or Swanlinbar or Lifford.

V

"It had always been my sense," I hear him still, "that the goat fades into the

goad

and the spur fades into the flank
and the fastness fades into no fixed abode

and the Black Pig's Dyke fades into the piggy bank
and your Hams fade into your Japheths
and the point fades into the point-blank

and the Cristal fades into the crystal meths
where the ends somehow begin to fade into the means
and the sheugh fades into the shibboleth

and the timbre fades into the tambourine
and the quiddity fades into the *quid pro quo*
and—you'll like this, I know—the bourne fades into the boreen."

MOY SAND AND GRAVEL

To come out of the Olympic Cinema and be taken aback
by how, in the time it took a dolly to travel
along its little track
to the point where two movie stars' heads
had come together smackety-smack
and their kiss filled the whole screen,

those two great towers directly across the road
at Moy Sand and Gravel
had already washed, at least once, what had flowed
or been dredged from the Blackwater's bed
and were washing it again, load by load,
as if washing might make it clean.

If and when I did look up, the sky over the Moy was the very same

                                             gray-blue

as the slow lift

of steam-smoke over the seam

of manure on a midwinter morning. I noticed the splash of red lead

on my left boot as again and again I would bend

my knee and bury my head in the rich

black earth the way an ostrich

was rumored to bury its head. My hands were blue

with cold. Again and again I would bend

to my left and lift

by one handle a creel of potatoes—King Edwards, gray as lead—

mined from what would surely seem

to any nine- or ten-year-old an inexhaustible seam.

My father wore a bag-apron that read, in capital letters, RICH.

My own capital idea, meanwhile, had sunk like a lead

balloon. "Blow all you like," my father turned on me. "Talk till you're blue

in the face. I won't let you take a lift

from the Monk. Blow all you like. I won't bend."

The Monk had spent twenty-odd years as a priest in South Bend,
his face priest-smooth except for a deep seam
in his left cheek. Fred Grew said something strange about how he liked to
"lift

his shirttail." Jack Grimley chipped in with how he was "ostrich-
sized" because he once lent Joe Corr a book called *Little Boy Blue.*
When Fred Grew remarked on his having "no lead

in his pencil," I heard myself say, cool as cool, "I think you've all been
misled."
At which the RICHARDSON'S TWO-SWARD suddenly began to unbend
in that distinctive pale blue
lettering as the seam
of his bag-apron unstitched itself and my father turned on me again:
"That's rich,

all right. If you think, after that, I'd let the Monk give you a lift

into the Moy to see Montgomery bloody Clift
you've another think coming. I'll give him two barrels full of twelve-gauge
lead
if he comes anywhere near you. Bloody popinjay. Peacock. *Ostrich.*"
All I could think of was how the Monk was now no more likely to show me
how to bend

that note on the guitar—"like opening a seam

straight into your heart"—when he played Bessie Smith's "Cold in Hand

Blues"

than an ostrich to bend

its lead-plumed wings and, with its two-toed foot, rip out the horizon seam

and lift off, somehow, into the blue.

THE BRAGGART

He sucked, he'll have you know,

the telltale sixth toe

of a woman who looked like a young Marilyn Monroe,

her hubby getting a little stroppy

when he found them there in the back of that old jalopy.

Other papers please copy.

THE WHINNY

When he veered into the mirror to fix his collar stud
he heard the whinny
of a stallion at stud,
saw the egg-yellow gloss in the coat of a young ass or hinny

or a pit pony's glossy forelock
not unlike his own. A stable lad had already tried to pick
the lock
on his near hind hoof. All spick-

and-span then, turned out in the yard,
with the prepuce
of his yard
an unprepossessing puce,

he knew he'd have to buck
the trend
of these stud collars, ordered from Sears Roebuck
at year's end

by one or other of his American "aunts,"
knew he'd have to surmount

the twits and taunts
of the stable lad who'd watched him mount

the dais, dressed to the nines,
to take the prize for Geography. "You can't tell, I'll own,
the Pennines from the Apennines,
you little shit-your-knickers,"

he heard the pit pony vet
him over his own shoulder, his voice now full-blown,
now fading into the velvet
among the other snorts and snickers.

A COLLEGELANDS CATECHISM

Which is known as the "Orchard County"?
Which as the "Garden State"?
Which captain of the *Bounty*
was set adrift by his mate?

Who cooked and ate an omelette
midway across Niagara Falls?
Where did Setanta get
those magical hurley balls

he ram-stammed down the throat
of the blacksmith's hound?
Why would a Greek philosopher of note
refuse to be bound

by convention but live in a tub
from which he might overhear,
as he went to rub
an apple on his sleeve, the mutineers

plotting to seize the *Maid of the Mist*
while it was still half able to forge
ahead and make half a fist
of crossing the Niagara gorge,

the tub in which he might light a stove
and fold the beaten
eggs into themselves? Who unearthed the egg-trove?
And who, having eaten

the omelette, would marvel at how the Mounties
had so quickly closed in on him, late
of the "Orchard County"
by way of the "Garden State"?

BEAGLES

That Boxing Day morning, I would hear the familiar, far-off gowls and
                                                                gulders
over Keenaghan and Aughanlig
of a pack of beagles, old dogs disinclined to chase a car suddenly quite
                                                                unlike
themselves, pups coming helter-skelter
across the plowlands with all the chutzpah of veterans
of the trenches, their slate-grays, cinnamons, liver-browns, lemons, rusts,
                                                                and violets
turning and twisting, unseen, across the fields,
their gowls and gulders turning and twisting after the twists and turns
of the great hare who had just now sauntered into the yard where I stood
                                                                on tiptoe
astride my new Raleigh cycle,
his demeanor somewhat louche, somewhat lackadaisical
under the circumstances, what with him standing on tiptoe
as if to mimic me, standing almost as tall as I, looking as if he might for a
                                                                moment put
himself in my place, thinking better of it, sloping off behind the lorry bed.

TELL

He opens the scullery door, and a sudden rush
of wind, as raw as raw,
brushes past him as he himself will brush
past the stacks of straw

that stood in earlier for Crow
or Comanche tepees hung with scalps
but tonight pass muster, row upon row,
for the foothills of the Alps.

He opens the door of the peeling shed
just as one of the apple peelers—
one of almost a score
of red-cheeked men who pare

and core
the red-cheeked apples for a few spare
shillings—mutters something about "bloodshed"
and the "peelers."

The red-cheeked men put down their knives
at one and the same

moment. All but his father, who somehow connives
to close one eye as if taking aim

or holding back a tear,
and shoots him a glance
he might take, as it whizzes past his ear,
for another Crow, or Comanche, lance

hurled through the Tilley-lit
gloom of the peeling shed,
were he not to hear what must be an apple split
above his head.

GUNS AND BUTTER

I

It seemed that Bap, who buried two milk churns
like two zigzaggy funerary urns
   between the posts of a gate,
would now be most likely to castigate
   me for daring to explode
   the myth of the mother lode.

II

It seemed that Biscuit, who rigged a tin
of cookies one night in Desertmartin,
   would now hold me in utter
contempt for daring to spread the butter
   meant to save his guns from rust
   on my small bit of a crust.

ONE LAST DRAW OF THE PIPE

Heard a piece of Roscommon folklore the other night. At some village or other, they lay pipes full of tobacco on the graves of the new burried in case they may like a draw of the pipe. A wild American indian kind of buisness it seems.
—A LETTER FROM W. B. YEATS TO DOUGLAS HYDE, OCTOBER 1889

Even though it happened as long ago as the late fifties, I could still draw
you a picture of the place. A little draw

through which we were helping a neighbor draw
green hay when we would suddenly draw

level with a freshly dug hole. He must have been torn between one last
                                                             draw
of the pipe and hurriedly trying to draw

a veil of thatch and pine boughs over the hole before having to withdraw,
that ghost who may even now draw

a bead on me. On the day Sitting Bull was shot, his old trick pony (once
                                                        such a draw
in Buffalo Bill's circus because he was given to dance

attendance

when he heard a volley of shots) would automatically draw

himself up and raise one hoof.

Even now I hear it coming down. I hear it coming down on my yew-bough

roof.

CAEDMON'S HYMN

Now we must praise to the skies,   the Keeper of the heavenly kingdom,
The might of the Measurer,   all he has in mind,
The work of the Father of Glory,   of all manner of marvel,

Our eternal Master,   the main mover.
It was he who first summoned up,   on our behalf,
Heaven as a roof,   the holy Maker.

Then this middle-earth,   the Watcher over humankind,
Our eternal Master,   would later assign
The precinct of men,   the Lord Almighty.

PAUL VALÉRY: *POMEGRANATES*

Thick-skinned pomegranates, your rinds
forced open by a rashness of seeds, you've led
me to envisage the highest foreheads
bursting with all that comes to mind.

Should all those suns you suffer,
O pomegranates with gaping sides,
leave you so swollen with pride
as to break down your ruby buffers,

should the wizened gold of your skin
give way to pressure from within
and explode in red juice-gems,

that light-shedding fracture
might bring a soul such as I had to dream
of its own hidden architecture.

PINEAPPLES AND POMEGRANATES

In memory of Yehuda Amichai

To think that, as a boy of thirteen, I would grapple
with my first pineapple,
its exposed breast
setting itself as another test
of my willpower, knowing in my bones
that it stood for something other than itself alone
while having absolutely no sense
of its being a worldwide symbol of munificence.
Munificence—right? Not munitions, if you understand
where I'm coming from. As if the open hand
might, for once, put paid
to the hand grenade
in one corner of the planet.
I'm talking about pineapples—right?—not pomegranates.

WINTER WHEAT

I

The plowboy was something his something as I nibbled the lobe
of her right ear and something her blouse
for the Empire-blotchy globe
of her left breast on which there something a something louse.

II

Those something lice like something seed pearls
and her collar something with dandruff
as when Queen Elizabeth entertained the Earls
in her something something ruff.

III

I might have something the something groan
of the something plowboy who would with such something urge
the something horses, a something and a roan,

had it not been for the something splurge

of something like the hare

which even now managed to something itself from the something

plowshare.

HERM

In memory of Ted Hughes

He stands in under the hedge, among the sweet-smelling flags,
and holds out a white flag
to the distant plow team
that makes directly for him through the teem

of rain, his head one of those plastered, round stones
atop a heap of pavers and kidney stones.
Or he might be a young holly or ash
what with his brow-beat of ash.

As the team bears down on him through the fertile
meadow, the white on the lead horse's forehead (like the white where a tile
once fell off the wall behind the range)
comes into range

and a priest with a handkerchief
reels among those mown down in Derry, whispering to him, "Chief . . ."
as he grips his wrist and starts counting,
"We were counting

on you to hold steady, to stay

our consolation and stay."

"But I've always taken my bearings from *you*," he'll hear himself remark,

"it was you I took for my mark."

WHITETHORNS

The paling posts we would tap into the ground with the flat of a spade
more than thirty years ago,
hammering them home then with a sledge
and stringing them with wire to keep our oats from Miller's barley,

are maxed out, multilayered whitethorns, affording us a broader, deeper
                                                                    shade
than we ever decently hoped to know,
so far-fetched does it seem, so far-flung from the hedge
under which we now sit down to parley.

AFFAIRS OF STATE

The lock of hair in a green-lined envelope
which was given to me by a woman with whom I planned to elope

in the mid-eighties came back, much to my disbelief,
as the single rusty leaf

like a rivet
in a thick hedge of boxwood or privet

along a drive like her front drive, now no more likely to disappoint
as it reached its vanishing point

in the hallway's missing tile
like a missing scale on a reptile

than when the previous owner, the diplomat,
had heard a green-lined envelope slither onto the mat

and, picking it up with a little *Oh,*
turned to his wife, the second one, the redhead, shortly to be his widow.

THE OTTER

That was the year S—— told him how on the Queen's desk

there lay a great six-by-four-foot blotter

of such a blackness, she would aver,

a blackness so dense

and a grain so close, so compact,

no one could hope to hold

a mirror up to it

and thereby . . . and thereby hit

on any evidence of clandestine contracts or covenants, of old

enemies having entered a secret pact

to which she might be a party or affix her hand, any evidence

of the treachery he now saw written all over her,

rising as she did to meet him like the otter

that had risen once to meet him from Lough Eske.

Believe you me, when I padded over the plowlands to the old Galloway

place

I was no less taken aback by the windowpane
covered not, as it had first seemed, with Carrickmacross lace

but a curtain of frost, than by the painter setting up his easel
in a meadow in Clonoe, or Clonmain,
my twitch as his badger and weasel

brushes twitched. Since this was still high summer, since the whin
vied with the cylinder of propane
for out-and-out yellowness, I assumed I had no more chance of getting in

than had Galloway of getting out, Galloway the blacksmith with his

crab-claw

of a right arm—as if he'd never had "but ane"—
Galloway who, in 1912, had stood in line at Balmoral to catch a glimpse of

Bonar Law.

ANTHONY GREEN: *THE SECOND MARRIAGE*

Standing as they do, all primped, primed, pukka, all proper, all property-
                                                              lined, in a room

where every rift's loaded with ore,

they're reminiscent less of a blushing bride and a nervous groom

than a pair of con artists summoned before

a magistrate inclined to throw

the book at con artists so that, despite his efforts to sustain

the argument that, as distinct from his previous situation in Rugby Row,

everything here hinges on his shadow meeting her shadow-stain

on the carpet, it looks very much as if, for Mr. Stanley Joscelyne and his
                                                                        mate,

the case will turn

rather on the provenance of a single inanimate

object—that silver cigarette urn,

it would appear, set on the occasional table

in the center of the room—and the outcome is, as he himself would put it,
                                                              "inevitable."

A S

As naught gives way to aught

and oxhide gives way to chain mail

and byrnie gives way to battle-ax

and Cavalier gives way to Roundhead

and Cromwell Road gives way to the Connaught

and *I Am Curious (Yellow)* gives way to *I Am Curious (Blue)*

and barrelhouse gives way to Frank'N'Stein

and a pint of Shelley plain to a pint of India Pale Ale

I give way to you.

As bass gives way to baritone

and hammock gives way to hummock

and Hoboken gives way to Hackensack

and bread gives way to reed bed

and bald eagle gives way to Theobald Wolfe Tone

and the Undertones give way to Siouxsie Sioux

and DeLorean, John, gives way to Deloria, Vine,

and Pierced Nose to Big Stomach

I give way to you.

As vent gives way to Ventry

and the King of the World gives way to Finn MacCool

and phone gives way to fax

and send gives way to sned

and Dagenham gives way to Coventry

and Covenanter gives way to caribou

and the caribou gives way to the carbine

and Boulud's cackamamie to the cock-a-leekie of Boole

I give way to you.

As transhumance gives way to trance

and shaman gives way to Santa

and butcher's string gives way to vacuum pack

and the ineffable gives way to the unsaid

and pyx gives way to monstrance

and treasure aisle gives way to need-blind pew

and Calvin gives way to Calvin Klein

and Town and Country Mice to Hanta

I give way to you.

As Hopi gives way to Navaho

and rug gives way to rag

and *Pax Vobiscum* gives way to Tampax

and Tampa gives way to the water bed

and *The Water Babies* gives way to *Worstward Ho*

and crapper gives way to loo

and spruce gives way to pine
and the carpet of pine needles to the carpetbag
I give way to you.

As gombeen-man gives way to not-for-profit
and soft soap gives way to Lynn C. Doyle
and tick gives way to tack
and Balaam's Ass gives way to Mister Ed
and *Songs of Innocence* gives way to *The Prophet*
and single-prop Bar-B-Q gives way to twin-screw
and the Salt Lick gives way to the County Line
and "Mending Wall" gives way to "Build Soil"
I give way to you.

As your hummus gives way to your foul madams
and your coy mistress gives way to "The Flea"
and flax gives way to W. D. Flackes
and the living give way to the dead
and John Hume gives way to Gerry Adams
and Television gives way to U2
and Lake Constance gives way to the Rhine
and the Rhine to the Zuider Zee
I give way to you.

As dutch treat gives way to french leave

and spanish fly gives way to Viagra

and slick gives way to slack

and the local fuzz give way to the Feds

and Machiavelli gives way to make-believe

and *Howards End* gives way to *A Room with a View*

and Wordsworth gives way to "Woodbine

Willie" and stereo Nagra to quad Niagara

I give way to you.

As cathedral gives way to cavern

and cookie cutter gives way to cookie

and the rookies give way to the All-Blacks

and the shad give way to the smoke shed

and the roughshod give way to the Black Horse avern

that still rings true

despite that T being missing from its sign

where a little nook gives way to a little nookie

when I give way to you.

That *Nanook of the North* should give way to *Man of Aran*

as ling gives way to cod

and cod gives way to kayak

and Camp Moosilauke gives way to Club Med

and catamite gives way to catamaran

and catamaran to aluminum canoe

is symptomatic of a more general decline

whereby a cloud succumbs to a clod

and I give way to you.

For as Monet gives way to Juan Gris

and Juan Gris gives way to Joan Miró

and Metro-Goldwyn-Mayer gives way to Miramax

and the Volta gives way to Travolta, swinging the red-hot lead,

and *Saturday Night Fever* gives way to *Grease*

and the Greeks give way to you know who

and the Roman IX gives way to the Arabic 9

and nine gives way, as ever, to zero

I give way to you.

THE STOIC

This was more like it, looking up to find a burlapped fawn
halfway across the iced-over canal, an Irish navvy who'd stood there for an

age

with his long-tailed shovel or broad griffawn,
whichever foot he dug with showing the bandage

that saved some wear and tear, though not so much that there wasn't a leak
of blood through the linen rag, a red picked up nicely by the turban
he sported, those reds lending a little brilliance to the bleak
scene of suburban or—let's face it—*urban*

sprawl, a very little brilliance. This was more like the afternoon last March
when I got your call in St. Louis and, rather than rave
as one might rant and rave at the thought of the yew
from Deirdre's not quite connecting with the yew from Naoise's grave,

rather than shudder like a bow of yew or the matchless Osage orange
at the thought of our child already lost from view
before it had quite come into range,
I steadied myself under the Gateway Arch

and squinted back, first of all, through an eyelet of bone
to a point where the Souris

had not as yet hooked up with the Assiniboine,

to where the Missouri

had not as yet been swollen by the Osage,

then ahead to where—let's face it—there are now *two* fawns

on the iced-over canal, two Irish navvies who've stood there for a veritable

age

with their long-tailed shovels or broad griffawns.

FAMOUS FIRST WORDS

Archimedes' first words were "Stand away from my diagram."
Sir Richard Burton's first word was "Chloroform."

Chang's first words were "I don't want to go to bed."
Alexandre Dumas's first words were "I shall never know how it all comes

out."

Thomas Edison's first words were "It is very beautiful over there."
John Ford's first words were "May I please have a cigar?"

Ulysses S. Grant's first word was "Water."
Prince Henry's first words were "I would say something but I cannot utter."

Washington Irving's first words were "When will this end?"
James Joyce's first words were "Does nobody understand?"

Ned Kelly's first words were "Such is life."
Saint Lawrence's first words were "This side is roasted enough."

Montezuma's first words were "I bear you no ill will."
Scipio Nasica's first words were "All is well with the general."

William Oughtred's first words were "Are you sure the king is restored?"

Elvis Presley's first words were "I hope you have not been bored."

General Alfredo Quijano's first words were "Still a little closer."

Maximilien de Robespierre's first words were "Thank you, sir."

Gertrude Stein's first words were "In that case, what's the question?"

Henry David Thoreau's first words were "Moose . . . Indian . . ."

Sir Thomas Urquhart's first word was something like
                    "Habonghadingdonghagong."

Leonardo da Vinci's first words were "God and man have I offended."

William III's first words were "Can this last long?"

Saint Francis Xavier's first words were "Let me never be confounded."

Jack B. Yeats's first words were "Don't forget your sitting."

Emile Zola's first words were "It must be something we've eaten."

THE GRAND CONVERSATION

She. My people came from Korelitz
where they grew yellow cucumbers
and studied the Talmud.
He. Mine pored over the mud
of mangold- and potato-pits
or flicked through kale plants from Comber
as bibliomancers of old
went a-flicking through deckle-mold.

She. Mine would lie low in the shtetl
when they heard the distant thunder
stolen by the Cossacks.
He. It was potato sacks
lumped together on a settle
mine found themselves lying under,
the Peep O'Day Boys from Loughgall
making Defenders of us all.

She. Mine once controlled the sugar trade
from the islets of Langerhans
and were granted the deed
to Charlottesville. *He.* Indeed?
My people called a spade a spade

and were admitted to the hanse
of pike- and pickax-men, shovels
leaning to their lean-to hovels.

She. Mine were trained to make a suture
after the bomb and the bombast
have done their very worst.
He. Between *fearsad* and *verst*
we may yet construct our future
as we've reconstructed our past
and cry out, my love, each to each
from his or her own quicken-queach.

She. Each from his stand of mountain ash
will cry out over valley farms
spotlit with pear blossom.
He. There some young Absalom
picks his way through cache after cache
of ammunition and small arms
hidden in grain wells, while his nag
tugs at a rein caught on a snag.

ON

Absalom was riding his mule and the mule passed under the thick branches of a great oak. Absalom's head got caught in the oak and he was left hanging between heaven and earth, while the mule he was riding went on.

—II SAMUEL 18:9

I make my way alone through the hand-to-hand fighting
to A3 and A5. Red velvet. Brass and oak.
The special effects will include strobe lighting
and artificial smoke.

A glance to A5. Patrons are reminded, *mar bheadh,*
that the management accepts no responsibility in the case of theft.
Even as the twenty-five-piece orchestra
that's masked offstage left

strikes up, there's still a chance, I suppose, that the gainsayers
might themselves be gainsaid
as you rush, breathless, into my field of vision.

Understudies and standbys never substitute for listed players,
however, unless a specific announcement is made.
There will be no intermission.

AN OLD PIT PONY

An old pit pony walks
its chalks
across a blasted heath.

Its coat is a cloud hung on a line.

It sighs
for the pit-propped skies
of that world beneath.

Its coat is a cloud hung on a line.

SUMMER COAL

I *GRIGGSTOWN, JUNE 1889*

Always the fence, always the row of bottles
lining the fence at the end of a garden
that runs down to the canal. From where we stand, on the barge,
it's like looking through a curtain

of magenta glass, or saffron with snuff-mottles,
or cobalt, or viridian,
in which a cottage now puckers, now is large
as life. We close one eye and think of our good fortune

compared to theirs, glad to know
we might as easily get the measure
of them as we do their bottles left for show

on a silver-gray cedar pole,
steadying ourselves and picking them off at our leisure
with lumps of coal.

It's like looking through a chink in wattle
and daub that has yet to harden,
through a scrim of feldspar-loaded sparge,
as two mule tenders come along the Delaware and Raritan

at something approaching full throttle.
These are mule tenders of my own age, thirteen or fourteen,
who may yet be conscripted to lead a charge
against Villa, to fall at Vimy or Verdun,

so eagerly they throw
themselves into their work. Little do they suspect that the pleasure
they take in their slow

bombardment might be surpassed by our own, as we fill the cellar hole
in which we store such treasure
with lumps of coal.

THE LOAF

When I put my finger to the hole they've cut for a dimmer switch
in a wall of plaster stiffened with horsehair
it seems I've scratched a two-hundred-year-old itch

with a pink and a pink and a pinkie-pick.

When I put my ear to the hole I'm suddenly aware
of spades and shovels turning up the gain
all the way from Raritan to the Delaware

with a clink and a clink and a clinky-click.

When I put my nose to the hole I smell the floodplain
of the canal after a hurricane
and the spots of green grass where thousands of Irish have lain

with a stink and a stink and a stinky-stick.

When I put my eye to the hole I see one holding horse dung to the rain
in the hope, indeed, indeed,
of washing out a few whole ears of grain

with a wink and a wink and a winkie-wick.

And when I do at last succeed

in putting my mouth to the horsehair-fringed niche

I can taste the small loaf of bread he baked from that whole seed

with a link and a link and a linky-lick.

THE OUTHOUSE

This would have been a night in late August,
somewhere in or around the turn of the century, when a little gust
bestirred itself from Lake Champlain
and he himself got up, as a dead man might get up, from where he'd lain

to find his way over that ever-treacherous rise
in the yard. Some version of the outhouse still stood and—surprise,
                                            surprise—
as he unbuttoned himself to answer this "call of nature"
he found himself staring straight at his own majuscule signature.

What with the slightly unhinged seat, the spiked news stories, the dead-dog
                                            scent
of lilac, the lemon-lye, what with the acidic and the alkaline
muddling on into one odor,

he knew in his bones that the crescent
moon would, for once, align
itself with the crescent moon cut high in the long-gone outhouse door.

NEWS HEADLINES FROM
THE HOMER NOBLE FARM

I

That case-hardened cop.
A bull moose in a boghole
brought him to a stop.

II

From his grassy knoll
he has you in his crosshairs,
the accomplice mole.

III

This sword once a share.
This forest a fresh-faced farm.
This stone once a stair.

IV

The birch crooks her arm,
as if somewhat more inclined
to welcome the swarm.

V

He has, you will find,
two modes only, the chipmunk:
fast-forward; rewind.

VI

The smell, like a skunk,
of coffee about to perk.
Thelonious Monk.

VII

They're the poker work
of some sort of woodpecker,
these holes in the bark.

VIII

My new fact checker
claims that *pilus* means "pestle."
My old fact checker.

IX

The Rose and Thistle.
Where the hummingbird drops in
to wet his whistle.

X

Behind the wood bin
a garter snake snaps itself,
showing us some skin.

XI

Like most bits of delf,
the turtle's seen at its best
on one's neighbor's shelf.

XII

Riding two abreast
on their stripped-down, souped-up bikes,
bears in leather vests.

XIII

The eye-shaded shrike.
BIRD BODIES BURIED IN BOG'S
a headline he'll spike.

XIV

Steady, like a log
riding a sawmill's spillway,
the steady coydog.

XV

The cornet he plays
was Bolden's, then Beiderbecke's,
this lonesome blue jay.

XVI

Some fresh auto wreck.
Slumped over a horn. Sump pool.
The frog's neck-braced neck.

XVII

Brillo pads? Steel wool?
The regurrrrrrrrrrrrrrrrrrrgitations, what,
of a long-eared owl?

XVIII

The jet with the jot.
The drive-in screen with the sky.
The blood with the blot.

XIX

How all seems to vie,
not just my sleeping laptop
with the first firefly.

THE KILLDEER

Why was he trying to clear
a space in the forest of beech
by turning beech posts and, by beech pegs,
fitting each to each?

For the reason at which the killdeer
seems to be clutching
when she lays her four pear-shaped eggs
with the pointed ends touching.

BOOK I ODE XV

While the young herdsman, Paris, a herdsman as faithless as he was fair,
was hauling Helen back on his boat
of Trojan pine, the sea-god Nereus would stop the sea-airs
that can't abide being stopped and float

this vision of the future: "It doesn't bode well that you've taken on deck
a woman whom the Greeks will band together and swear an oath
to recover by force, determined as they'll be to wreck
your marriage and old Priam's kingdom both,

and I dread to think of the sweat-drenched horses, the men drenched with
                                                                    sweat,
dread to think of the carnage
you're visiting on Troy. Even now Athena is laying out her breastplate and
                                                                    helmet,
limbering up her battle carriage and battle rage.

However confident you may be about coming under Venus's special care,
there'll be no point in pretending to groom
your long hair while from your measured lyre you pluck the measured airs
the ladies seem to go for. There'll be no point in hiding out in the bedroom

to avoid the heavy throwing-spears and Cretan arrowheads,
what with Ajax hard on your heels, what with the rumpus and ruck
of battle. Then you may dread
to think, after all, of your long hair dragged through the muck.

Can't you make out Ulysses, sworn enemy of your people, at your back?
Nestor of Pylos coming after you?
Teucer of Salamis hot on your tracks?
Not to speak of Sthenelus, who knows a thing or two

about handling himself in a fight, not to speak
of handling a chariot team.
Meriones is yet another Greek
with whom you'll be all too familiar. Diomedes also, whom some deem

deadlier than his father, Tydeus, is following in your wake,
and when you sight him, like a stag sighting a wolf on the opposite hillside,
you'll soon forget grass nibbling and take off, head thrown back, breathless,
                                                    all aquake—
hardly what she thought was coming to her, your bride.

For though Achilles and his fleet, consumed as they are with ire,

may delay the course of events, by the time ten years have rolled round

the Greeks will have set the fire

that will burn Troy to the ground."

BOOK III ODE XVIII

Faunus, you who love the nymphs, from whom the nymphs love to run,

may you look kindly, as you cross in and out of my farm,

on its boundary posts and pastures already blessed by the sun,

and deliver the littlest of my flock from harm

if it please you that, at the high point of the year,

a little kid might indeed be offered to you, the wine

which Venus holds so dear

indeed fill the mixing bowl, smoke rise from the ancient shrine,

one and all besporting themselves on the still-green grazing

as early December rolls round, be it the flocks

of sheep or the country folk lazing

with the lazing ox,

the wolf moving among lambs remarkable for their nonchalance,

the trees putting out their red

carpet for you, or the ditchdigger dancing a three-step victory dance

on the earth with which he's gone head-to-head.

EUGENIO MONTALE: *THE EEL*

The selfsame, the siren
of icy waters, shrugging off as she does the Baltic
to hang out in our seas,
our inlets, the rivers
through which she climbs, bed-hugger, who keeps going against
the flow, from branch to branch, then
from capillary to snagged capillary,
farther and farther in, deeper and deeper into the heart
of the rock, straining
through mud runnels, till one day
a flash of light from the chestnut trees
sends a fizzle through a standing well,
through a drain that goes
by dips and darts from the Apennines to the Romagna—
that selfsame eel, a firebrand now, a scourge,
the arrow shaft of Love on earth
which only the gulches or dried-out
gullies of the Pyrenees might fetch and ferry back
to some green and pleasant spawning ground,
a green soul scouting and scanning
for life where only
drought and desolation have hitherto clamped down,
the spark announcing

that all sets forth when all that's set forth

is a charred thing, a buried stump,

this short-lived rainbow, its twin met

in what's set there between your eyelashes,

you who keep glowing as you do, undiminished, among the sons

of man, faces glistening with your slime, can't you take in

her being your next-of-kin?

WHEN AIFRIC AND I PUT IN AT THAT LITTLE CREEK

When Aifric and I put in at that little creek
in the shadow of Masatiompan
what struck me most was not the view. What struck me most
was the reek
as from the copper pan

her father would pore over each and every morning, the ravel
of straw-strain and honey-strand
as he leaned against the tiller post
and winced at his own kidney gravel.
When our little boat lurched toward the strand

Aifric herself lurched, and I was fortunate in being able,
on account of the riding up of her Aran
sweater that seemed to boast
not only "diamond" and "cable"
but "basket" stitches, to glimpse the spot where the colors ran

red and black. For though our sonar was pretty much state of the art,
the truth is that we had found our way back
along this coast
largely by means of the chart
her father had drawn and redrawn on Aifric's back

with nothing more than a bronze pin

and lamp soot and red ocher, the constant twinge and tweak

of detail with which he had been so engrossed

when he suddenly caught the swing of the boom and took that fatal spin

only the previous week.

THE ANCESTOR

The great-grandmother who bears down on us, as if beholding the mote
in our eye, from a nineteenth-century Hungarian portrait
on our library wall is no relation. Not even remote.
The straw-hatted man in a daguerreotype, though he and I may share the
                                                                    trait

of putting two fingers to the little carbuncle
on our right chin, is no more of my blood than I am
consanguineous with Cromwell. Our Webster's is inscribed "Philip. Best
                                                                uncle."
Our napkins bear an unfamiliar monogram.

Yet how familiar all become. Shaving mug, gymkhana rosette, five charms
from a charm bracelet—all those heirlooms
to which we're now the heirs are at once more presentable and

more present than our own. This great-grandmother with folded arms
who lurches and looms
across the library may not be so unreasoning in her reprimand.

HOMESICKNESS

The lion stretched like a sandstone lion on the sandstone slab
of a bridge with one fixture, a gaslight,
looks up from his nicotine-worried forepaw
with the very same air my father, Patrick,
had when the results came back from the lab,
that air of anguish-awe
that comes with the realization of just how slight
the chances are of anything doing the trick

as the sun goes down over Ballyknick and Ballymacnab
and a black-winged angel takes flight.

The black-winged angel leaning over the sandstone parapet
of the bridge wears a business suit, dark gray.
His hair is slick with pomade.
He turns away as my mother, Brigid,
turned away from not only her sandstone pet
but any concession being made.
The black-winged angel sets her face to the unbending last ray
of evening and meets rigid with rigid

as the sun goes down over Lisnagat and Listamlet
and Clonmore and Clintyclay.

Feckless as he was feckless, as likely as her to be in a foofaraw,

I have it in me to absolutely rant and rail while, for fear of the backlash,

absolutely renounce

the idea of holding anything that might be construed as an opinion.

The lion still looks back to his raw

knuckle and sighs for the possibility that an ounce

of Walnut Plug might shape up from the ash.

The angel still threatens to abandon us with a single flick of her pinion

as the sun goes down over Lislasly and Lissaraw

and Derrytrasna and Derrymacash.

TWO STABS AT OSCAR

I

As I roved out between a gaol
and a river in spate
in June as like as January
I happened on a gate
which, though it lay wide open,
would make me hesitate.

I was so long a prisoner
that, though I now am free,
the thought that I serve some sentence
is so ingrained in me
that I still wait for a warder
to come and turn the key.

II

A stone breaker on his stone bed
lay no less tightly curled

than opposite-leaved saxifrage

that even now, unfurled,

has broken through its wall of walls

into this other world.

THE BREATHER

Think of this gravestone
as a long, low chair
strategically placed
at a turn in the stair.

THE GOOSE

I

When Hermes gave that bit of a goose to the goose farmer
it not only laid an egg
packed with gold but its leg
was a scaled-down version of a knight's in armor,

its beak done in a pinch
of gold so fine it might have been beaten by some master gilder
described by Pliny the Elder,
give or take a thousandth of an inch.

II

About as deep, then, as the melanoma
they diagnosed in one old friend, so taking it upon themselves to dig
a hole in her as long as the main street in Omagh.

III

As if they hadn't already made enough room—

for *whatever* it is—when they went after another's ovaries and womb.

Yesterday she drove down to Newry to buy a bit of a wig.

A BRIEF DISCOURSE ON DECOMMISSIONING

I stood between Biscuit and Bap
    in the mortar-mixed gap
to the field where they put the lid
    on that great pyramid
we'd built about a musket stack
    as Bap laid down the law:
you can't make bricks without the straw
    that breaks the camel's back.

THE TURN

In those days when the sands
might shift at any moment, when his mother might at any moment lay
into him, he thought nothing of getting up halfway through a story about
the Sahara,
the one about the tribesman following the scent
of water to a water hole, thought nothing of getting up and going out
while he was still halfway through a sentence, going out and taking a turn

about the house, sometimes not bothering to return
for an hour, two hours, a week, a year perhaps, perhaps not until the sands
of time had run out,
not until his favorite guinea hen had brought herself to lay
a double-yolked egg, or the double scent
of the sandpile and the dunghill made a Sahara

of the yard through which Ned Skinner had moaned "Saahaara, Saahaara,"
the yard in which, after seeing *The Four Feathers*, he'd taken it upon himself
to turn
a stack of pear boxes still redolent of the scent
of pears into a bolster-humped camel that carried him across the endless
sands
to where Harry Feversham and himself lay
in wait in a gully for the last of those out-and-out

cowards and scoundrels, the yard in which he'd not only learned to spout
most, if not all, of the main languages of the Sahara
but had such a grasp of the lay
of the land, every twist and turn
of the ergs and regs which looked for all the world like featureless sands,
had so mastered following the scent

of water to a water hole, shielding his eyes from the henhouse's fluorescent
strip of light, under which he could make out a couple making out
in a featureless room in the old Sands,
or a featureless room in the Sahara,
a light by which he could make out every twist and turn
in what would have seemed to a lay

person a featureless hotel room, a room which offered him an instant
                                                              replay
of the old bolster and pear-box scent
rising from the camel under him, a scent powerful enough to turn
him around, reminding him that he'd already been out
for an hour, two hours, a week, a year perhaps, having him turn back
                                                    through the Sahara
in which so many had perished, back through the sands

on which lay the bones of thousands

of his countrymen, through the sandpile that was not at all reminiscent of

the Sahara,

having him turn back inside to pick up his own sentence, to hear himself

out.

REDKNOTS

The day our son is due is the very day
the redknots are meant to touch down
on their long haul
from Chile to the Arctic Circle,
where they'll nest on the tundra
within a few feet
of where they were hatched.
Forty or fifty thousand of them
are meant to drop in along Delaware Bay.

They time their arrival on these shores
to coincide with the horseshoe crabs
laying their eggs in the sand.
Smallish birds to begin with,
the redknots have now lost half their weight.
Eating the eggs of the horseshoe crabs
is what gives them the strength to go on,
forty or fifty thousand of them getting up all at once
as if for a rock concert encore.

CRADLE SONG FOR ASHER

When they cut your birth cord yesterday
it was I who drifted away.

Now I hear your name (in Hebrew, "blest")
as yet another release of ballast

and see, beyond your wicker
gondola, campfires, cities, whole continents flicker.

Awesome, the morning after Hurricane Floyd, to sit out in our driveway

and gawk

at yet another canoe or kayak

coming down Canal Road, now under ten feet of water. We've wheeled to

the brim

the old Biltrite pram

in which, wrapped in a shawl of Carrickmacross

lace and a bonnet

of his great-grandmother Sophie's finest needlepoint,

Asher sleeps on, as likely as any of us to find a way across

the millrace on which logs (trees more than logs)

are borne along, to which the houses down by the old Griggstown Locks

have given up their inventory.

I'm happy for once to be left high and dry,

happy that the house I may yet bring myself to call mine

is set on a two-hundred-and-fifty-year-old slab,

happy that, if need be, we might bundle a few belongings into a pillow slip

and climb the hill and escape, Please Examine

Your Change, to a place where the soul might indeed recover

radical innocence. A police launch maneuvering by brought back troops on

maneuver,

some child-kin of my children dipping a stale

crust in his bowl of kale

while listening to his parents complain about the cost

of running a household

in the Poland of the 1930s, the child who, Please Hold,

a peaked cap would shortly accost

for the whereabouts of his uncle, the sofer.

Awesome, however stormy yesterday's weather, to calmly don a safari

hat that somewhat matches my safari coat

and, determined as I am to make the most of the power cut

here on Ararat,

tear another leaf from Edward Bulwer-Lytton's

King Poppy to light the barbecue, the barbecue shortly to be laden

with Dorothy's favorite medallions of young rat

and white-lipped peccary taken this morning not with old-fashioned piano

wire

but the latest in traps. I'll rake the ashes of the fire

on which they'll cook, No Turn

On Red, and watch the Mediterranean

do its level best to meet the "Caribbon,"

as Dorothy pronounced it once, on Canal Road, No Way Out,

having taken down from the attic the ancient Underwood
with the one remaining black ribbon

and set up shop in a corner of the garage.
When we wheeled the old Biltrite baby carriage
to the brink this morning, I was awestruck to see in Asher's glabrous
face a slew of interlopers
not from Maghery, as I might have expected, or Maghera, or Magherafelt
(though my connections there are now few and far between),
but the likes of that kale-eating child on whom the peaked cap, *Verboten*,
would shortly pin a star of yellow felt,

having accosted him on the Mosaic
proscription, Please Secure Your Own Oxygen Mask
Before Attending to Children, on the eating of white-lipped peccary.
Just one step ahead of the police launch, meanwhile, a 1920 Studebaker
had come down Canal Road, Do Not Fill
Above This Line, carrying another relative, Arnold Rothstein, the brain
behind the running, during Prohibition, of grain
alcohol into the States, his shirt the very same Day-Glo green of
                                        chlorophyll

on the surface of a cattle bath

or the canal itself, the canal that ordinarily reflects berm bank and towpath

as calm as calm. Jean had been fixing Asher a little gruel

from leftover cereal

and crumbled Zwieback

when Uncle Arnie came floating by the "nursery."

This was the Arnold Rothstein who had himself fixed the 1919 World

Series

by bribing eight Chicago White Sox players, Keep Back

Fifty Feet, to throw the game. So awestruck were we by his Day-Glo

shirt we barely noticed how low

in the water his Studebaker lay, the distribution of its cargo of grain

alcohol

(filtered through a makeshift charcoal-

packed, double downspout

by an accomplice, Waxey Gordon) somewhat less than even.

"The peccary's hind foot," the peaked cap would inquire, "you call that

cloven?"

Asher slept on, his little pout

set off beautifully by the pillowcase

into which we might yet bundle the foul madams, the couscous, the tabouleh carryout

full of grit

from the Sahara, while Uncle Arnie had taken his lawyer's advice,

maintaining that he paid none of the eight White Sox

who stood in the witness box

as much as a nickel. Racketeering, maybe. Extortion, maybe. Maybe vice.

But not throwing games. It wasn't an area in which he had expertise. Not

                                                    an expert.

Isaac Wolf of New Haven, meanwhile, had unzippered

a freezer bag and made a dent

in the defrosted dough in which we'd meant

to wrap the loin of peccary, Please Use Tongs,

in an Aussie version of the secret

recipe the Duke of Wellington had secured

from the Killadar of Perinda, one which substituted quantongs

for apricots. While Asher slept on, half hid

under the cradle hood,

his great-grandfather Jim Zabin, an adman who held, of all things, the

                                                    Biltrite account,

Please Examine Your Change As Mistakes Cannot,

nodded from his deathbed to the red

stain on the muslin cloth

that covered the peccary in its autoclave

as if that cloth were an obstacle whereby the haystack- and roof-leveling

wind, bred

on the Atlantic, might at last

be stayed. "By which authority," another great-grandfather, Sam Korelitz,

would blast

from his hardware store in Lawrence, Mass., "did you deny Asher a bris?"

A chain saw had let rip. Our next-door neighbor, Bruce,

was making quite a hand

of amputating a sycamore limb that had given its all

to the wind and rain. Asher slept on, his shawl

of Carrickmacross lace, his bonnet tied with silk reputed to come from

Samarkhand,

while Dorothy stood where the Delaware and Raritan Canal and the

Millstone

River combined to carry ton upon ton

of clay, hay, hair, shoes, spectacles, Please Use The Hammer To Break

The Glass, playing ducks and drakes

with the child-kin shortly to be riven

from her family and I, the so-called Goy from the Moy,

scrubbed the trap made in Marengo, Illinois,

by which we took that white-lipped peccary, as if scrubbing might leave me

shriven.

A flicker from behind Asher's sleeping lids, all covered with little wheals

and whelks,

as Jean's distant cousin, Helene Hanff, began to rub a mix of cumin and

baby talc

(cornstarch more than talc) into another loin

of peccary, this being a trick Helene

had picked up from the individual who started a trend

by keeping a rabbit warren–

cum-dovecote in a mews off Charing Cross Road, Hard Hats Must Be

Worn,

an individual who picked it up from whichever Waugh deemed a pram in

the hallway the end

of art, a Waugh who could no doubt trace it back to Wellington and the

Killadar

of Perinda. I looked up in dismay as the helter-skelter

I'd raised in lieu of a lonely tower (part float, part floating derrick)

was nudged by the millrace. The increasingly eccentric

Helene, meanwhile, continued to rub

cornstarch into the remains

of whatever curled in the autoclave. Almost inaudible now, the sycamore

moans

as, almost inaudibly, I myself continued to scrub

the latest in traps with a wire brush

from Sam's hardware store in Lawrence, Mass. "You ignore the Midrash

by which authority?" I could hear small incendiary

devices going off in the midst of the pleasantries

exchanged at this, as every, family gathering, Please Do Not Leave Window

Ajar,

where the stricken

face of Uncle Arnie's friend Fanny Brice peeked from her astrakhan.

"According to Horace," Arnie maintained, "every water pitcher started out

as a wine jar.

You may take Fanny for a nincompoop,

but I fear she may well be the only one here who's actually read *King Poppy*.

I fear, moreover, the way the smoke flings

and flails itself from your barbecue brings back that terrible morning, in

Sing Sing,

they fried Charlie Becker." Helene looked up from her cumin

splitting while Bruce began to pulverize

a stand of young sassafras

with all the zeal of a chain saw catechumen

and the groundbreaking Irish navvies continued to keen and kvetch

through the hole cut for a dimmer switch

in a wall of deh-dah stiffened with deh-dah. Next to moor

his little punt at our dock was Joe Hanff, the banker who helped Louis B.

Mayer

and Thomas Edison develop a "cool" projection lamp. Where he'd come by

the Coke and bucket

of popcorn God only knows.

He handed them to Dorothy for safekeeping while he concentrated on the

minutiae

of the peccary trap and the great trebucket

with which we've been known to take even larger critters,

setting and upsetting the trebucket as would an obsessive compulsive, Out

Of Order,

until he was himself ousted by Sam,

Sam who repeated the opening phrase (" *'asherey ha 'ish 'asher*") of the

Book of Psalms

as he handed Asher a Berbecker and Rowland

upholstery nail which Asher held as grim as grim

while sleeping on. Ton upon ton of clay, hay, hair, shoes, and spectacle

                                                                        frames

made it less and less likely that we would land

on our feet on the Griggstown Causeway any time soon, Ramp Divides,

Please Examine Your Change As Mistakes Cannot Be Rectified,

the almost inaudible roar

of the millrace drowning out a great-grandfather's prayer.

By which authority did we deny Asher a mohel?

By which authority did we deny Asher a rebbe?

Asher, meanwhile, slept on, his most crape-creepered of cribs

riding out the torrent, riding out the turmoil

of those thousands of Irish navvies piling clay, hay, hair into their creels

and bearing them at shoulder height, or above, with all the zeal

of creel catechumens. A tattoo on the left forearm

of some child-kin of my children, a very faint tattoo. Once more the storm

was howling and something, deh-dah, deh-dah,

something about that clay and hair going down the sluice

brought back an afternoon in St. Louis.

Something about raking the ashes of the barbecue at the end of the

                                                                        verandah

and turning over the loin and flank

of a young peccary, its loin so lean and lank,

its little rib cage, Road Narrows.

Something about turning over that runt of the peccary farrow,

with a dink and a dink

and a dinky-dick, brought back that afternoon. Something about Sam

lighting a menorah

and reading a commentary on the Torah,

something about Arnie distancing himself from the "night-and-fog" of

Murder Inc.

to a disbelieving Duke of Wellington and Killadar of Perinda,

brought back the day

of our own *Nacht-und-Nebel Erlass*

on which I'd steadied myself under the Gateway Arch and pondered the

loss

of our child. It was Arnie who'd been the brain behind running rum

to those thousands of Irish schlemiels

who dug the canal. A flicker from Asher's lids. The little whelks and wheals.

As if he might be dreaming of a Pina Colostrum

on Boscobel Beach, some young beauty dipping his foot in Johnson's baby

oil.

Fanny peeked from her astrakhan, its poile

the poile of a stillborn lamb. Again a chain saw letting rip.

Again I scrubbed the very latest in traps

while Helene rubbed cornstarch into whatever was curled, rawer and rawer,

in the autoclave. "That peccary with the hind foot,"

the peaked cap would inquire, "it's a bad case of spina bifida?"

I heard a bottom drawer

open somewhere. The red stain on the lint

that covered whatever it was in the autoclave brought back an afternoon in

Poland

when the smoke would flail and fling itself, Maximum Headroom,

from a crematorium

at Auschwitz. It was not without some

trepidation, so, that I trained my camcorder

on this group of creel carters

bearing clay, hay, hair (at shoulder height, or above) through the awesome

morning after Hurricane Floyd as yet another 1921 Benz or 1924 Bugatti

came down Canal Road and yet another peaked

cap was enquiring of my child-kin the meaning of "Ashkenaz,"

Place Mask over Mouth and Nose,

my trepidation becoming more and more

pronounced as that smoke would flail and fling itself over Auschwitz.

I looked up from our make-believe version of Boscobel Beach

to a cauterized stump of sassafras or sycamore

as the creel carters piled more and more clay, hay, hair, spectacle frames,

Willkommen,

onto the line of carrioles and camions

by the edge of the flooded stream, those creel carters imagining in excited

reverie

the arches of the bridge wrought with the motto *Arbeit Macht Frei,*

while I looked up through the swing

and swale of smoke, Please Leave a Message after the Beep,

and watched the kebab-babby we had lost a year or two back put on its

best bib

and tucker, watched it put out its little bit of a wing

all tinged with char

as if to set off for the real Boscobel Beach (on which we had met Sandra

Hughes and Anton Hajjar),

oblivious to the piles of hair, spectacle frames, bootees and brogans

borne along from wherever. "The full name is Auschwitz-Birkenau,"

Sam was explaining to Anton and Sandra,

who had somehow summoned themselves. Asher slept on, of course,

despite his thrush,

despite his diaper rash,

the floodwater having receded from the point on the driveway at which the

pachysandra

had earlier been swamped, the point at which Arnie had fixed some class of

a tow rope

to the chassis of the Studebaker. "I simply don't have it in me to bribe

a ballplayer," he would main-

tain, steadying himself with a handful of mane

as he hooked the rope to the hames of a draft mule, This Truck

Makes Wide Right Turns. The fact that the slew of interlocutors

in Asher's glabrous face now included, of all things, the peccary runt, Do

Not Litter,

left me no less awestruck

than if the Studebaker were to be suddenly yanked back to the factory in

South Bend

from which it had been packed off, Open This End,

than if the soul of one of the dozen stillborn

lambs sewn into Fanny's astrakhan were to recover radical innocence and
learn,

than if scouring the trap by which I had taken that peccary, so lank and
lean,

by its dinky hind leg,

Don't Walk, than if, Don't Walk, than if, Don't Walk,

than if scouring might make it clean.

An overwhelming sense of déjà vu. The creel caravan

swaying along the salt route into Timbuktu. Fanny taking up a hand-held
microphone

and embarking on "Secondhand Rose." The convoy

of salt merchants setting down their loys

at one and the same moment. Our piliated woodpecker tapping at the bark

of three successive sycamores in the hope of finding one in tune.

The piles of clay, hay, hair, spectacle frames, hand-me-down

bootees and brogans now loaded onto the ark

causing it to lie so much lower in the water that Uncle Arnie gives a heavy
hint

to Fanny that she should cut the chorus of "Secondhand

Rose" and jump ship. "The whitewall

tire," Helene concurs, "is the beginning of the pram in the hall."

Asher sleeps on, attended by two Teddy bears,

his soul less likely than ever to recover radical innocence and learn at last

that it is self-delighting. Ada Korelitz, Sam's widow, is drawing up A-, B-,

and C-lists

of the Korelitz forebears

whom she'll invite to a reception thrown by herself and Arnie, Unapproved

Road,

for the 1919 World Series–winning Cincinnati Reds.

"If there's no hatred in a mind," Isaac Wolf

pounds and expounds, "assault and battery of the wind can never tear the

deh-dah from the leaf."

"As for the killdeer," Helene peeks from an astrakhan almost as natty

as Fanny's, "you're thinking, in all likelihood,

of the killdeer of Perinda." The ark now lies so much lower in the water,

Stop Ahead,

that Uncle Arnie gives another heavy hint to the Cincinnati

Reds that they should also jump ship, *Achtung*.

The 1920 Studebaker's just one step ahead of a Panther tank

nodding approvingly through the ghetto after the Germans have massacred
the Jews of Bialystok. The wind bred on the Atlantic has broken Belmar
and Seagirt.

Boundbrook is broken. The roof-leveling wind, profane and irreverent,
the wind which was at the spearhead
of the attack on the ark, almost inaudible. The memory of a three-month
growth spurt

no more than a flicker, For Rent,

behind Asher's sleeping lids. The A-, B-, and C-lists of forebears in his
glabrous face.

Hanff. Wolf. Reinhart. Abrams. A Reinhart beginning to fuss
as a peaked cap inquires about the Orthodox
position on the eating of white-lipped peccary. The train stopped in
Bialystok's

running neither to Warsaw nor Leningrad.
Helene uttering a little cuss
as the yellow of that star brings back the out-and-out yellowness of a
cylinder of gas

she once saw on Charing Cross Road. Now Isaac Wolf, a Yale grad,

looks on helplessly at the millrace on which signpost, signboard, Birdseed,
Keep Out,

Bridge Freezes Before Road, Do Not Drive in Breakdown Lane, Live Bait,
my lonely helter-skelter, $500 Fine,
the makeshift oven
in which we meant, Keep Clear, All Directions, the Vermont decal
on that Bugatti-load of grain alcohol, Slow,
the out-and-out yellow
of the signpost that points toward the place where the soul might recover
radical

innocence, No Stopping Except for Repairs, the makeshift oven in which
we meant to bake
the peccary *en croute*, Contents Under Pressure, the freezer bag
into which we've bundled the carryout from the Sahara,
the signpost that points to where the Missouri
had not as yet been swollen, Hump, No Shoulder, No Rail,
are all borne along, Toll Booth,
to where Uncle Arnie's father, Abraham Rothstein, one of the founders of
Beth
Israel (yes, *Beth Israel*),

joins Fanny Brice in the version of "My Man" she first sang in the *Ziegfeld
Follies.*
A flicker from behind the lids. As if those children-kin might flee

as they fled the Cossacks in the Ukraine,

Please Remember to Take Your Belongings When You Leave the Train,

woken as they now are by a piliated Rowland and Berbecker

tapping into a sycamore. Asher's face a fox's mask

nailed to a long-gone doorpost by an Irish schlemiel as likely as not to

mosk

his brogans for a ladle of rum. "What's with these police captains, like

Charlie Becker,"

Arnie puts his arm around Helene, who, being chosen, finds life flat,

Contents May Have Shifted During Flight,

"who think they're above the law, who think they're born without belly

buttons?"

The police launch maneuvering by brings back riot shields and batons,

some child-kin of my children picking at his kohlrabi.

Now Helene leaves off rubbing cornstarch

into the arch

of whatever lies in the autoclave, sets the little beak of her Colibri

wobblingly to a cigarette, Pull to Open,

and reaches into a drawer for the poultry shears. The hacking through a

babby bone.

No obstacle but Gregory's wood

and one bare hill, Slippery When Wet,

bringing back the morning Dr. Patel had systematically drawn

the child from Jean's womb, For Hire,

Uncle Arnie all the while hanging a whitewall tire

about the draft mule's neck, the draft mule no less thraward-thrawn

than whichever Waugh deemed the pram in the hallway the end of art.

The peaked cap sweet-talking that young Abrams or Reinhart

with the offer of a tin of waffeletten

should he feel able to enlighten

him on the particular house in the Bialystok ghetto

in which his uncle is hunkering down. Asher puts his lips to the shofar

of a long-gone pacifier

as Isaac Wolf expounds to Fanny Brice ("it's from *getto*, 'a foundry,' not

borghetto,

a 'borough' "), on that little gore, that little gusset

of ground into which my cast

of thousands of Irish schmucks have been herded, *Halt.*

Asher opens his eyes. Once more the storm is howling as it howled

when Isaac shouted down the board of Yale, the Black Horse Tavern still

served ale,

when Sophie was found dead in the bath, a ringed plover

with all her rings stolen, Please Cover,

when Sam discontinued his line of Berbecker and Rowland upholstery

nails, For Sale,

when we might yet have climbed the hill and escaped by Coppermine,

when Uncle Arnie was gut-shot (by George McManus?)

for nonpayment of tight-lipped, poker-faced debts, when Helene Hanff, the

celeb,

was found asleep

in the De Witt Nursing Home in the arms of Bulwer-Lytton, Follow

Detour,

when Fanny tried to stop the leak

of a so-called confession by one Joseph Gluck

which fingered her ex-husband, Nicky Arnstein, when the trebucket of my

lonely *túr*

was tripped for the very last time by Joe Hanff, No Egress,

when a cantankerous

young Reinhart or Abrams, No Children Beyond This Point,

was borne along at shoulder height by the peaked cap, Out of Bounds,

when the cry went up from a starving Irish schlemiel who washed an

endosperm

of wheat, deh-dah, from a pile of horse keek

held to the rain, one of those thousands of Irish schmucks who still loll,

still loll and lollygag,

between the preposterous towpath and the preposterous berm.

ACKNOWLEDGMENTS

Acknowledgments are due to the editors of:

The American Scholar, Avocado, Daedalus, Fulcrum, The Guardian, The Honest Ulsterman, The Irish Times, The Kenyon Review, Kestrel, The KGB Bar Book of Poems, London Magazine, The London Review of Books, magma, The Nassau Weekly, The New Delta Review, New Writing 8, The New York Review of Books, Notre Dame Review, The Observer, One Trick Pony, Ploughshares, Poetry Review, Quarterly West, The Recorder, River City, Samizdat, The Shop, Stand, The Sunday Times (London), *Thumbscrew, The Times Literary Supplement, Time's Tidings, Translation Ireland, Troubadour, US1, Washington Square,* and *The Yale Journal of Criticism.*

"The Ancestor," "The Grand Conversation," "News Headlines from the Homer Noble Farm," and "When Aifric and I Put In at That Little Creek" first appeared in *The New Yorker.*

"Hard Drive" was privately printed by the Gallery Press in December 1998, "John Luke: *The Fox*" in December 1999, "Beagles" in December 2000, "Horace: *Book III Ode XVIII*" in December 2001. "Unapproved Road" was commissioned for *The Border: Personal Reflections from Ireland, North and South,* published by Oak Tree Press. "Hard Drive" and "Unapproved Road" appeared in *Unapproved Road,* a limited edition with intaglio prints by Diarmuid Delargy, published by Pied Oxen. The translation of "Caedmon's Hymn" was made for Poems on the Underground, "Paul Valéry: *Pomegranates*" for *The Faber Book of Twentieth Century French Poetry,* "Horace: *Two Odes*" for *Horace, The Odes: New Translations by Contemporary Poets,* published by Princeton University Press, and "Eugenio Montale: *The Eel*" for *The Faber Book of Twentieth Century Italian Poetry.* "Herm" was included in *The Epic Poise: A Celebration of Ted Hughes,* published by Faber and Faber. "Anthony Green: *The Second Marriage*" appeared in *A Conversation Piece,* an anthology of poems about paintings in the Ulster Museum collection published by Abbey Press. A shortened version of "As" was broadcast on RTE Television on December 31, 1999 ("Millennium Eve"), while "The Stoic" was commissioned by the BBC World Service for "The Lyrics." "News Headlines from the Homer Noble Farm" was included in *Last Before America: Essays and Poems in Honour of Michael Allen,* published by the Blackstaff Press. "Two Stabs at Oscar" was commissioned by Reading Borough Council to be incorporated in the Oscar Wilde Memorial Walk, while "The Breather" was written for the 1999 Salisbury Festival and published by Picador in *Last Words.*

9 780374 528843